Found Guilty

My 26 Year Journey To Redemption

By

Dr. Antoinette M. Glenn

Published by Write the Book Now, an imprint of Perfect Time SHP LLC.

ISBN- 978-1-7361028-4-8

FOREWORD

When my mother went to prison, I was two years old. When she was released, I was seven turning eight. Imagine waking up and your mother was gone, never to return until over five years later. I remember waking up in the middle of the night. I got up out of bed, looking for my mother. I pulled the dining room chair to the door. I unlocked the bottom lock, but I knew there was another lock up higher that Grandma and Pop used to turn to open the door. Once I turned the knob, I got down off the chair and opened the door, but a chain stopped me from going out.

I began yelling, "Mommy, Mommy!" Grandma woke up and came into the living room. There I stood with the door open, yelling for my mommy and crying, but she never came; she was in prison.

I remember going to visit her and counting down the days until she came home. I remember asking her if I could come to spend the night with her. I remember being sad when she told me, "Just a little while longer."

I was so excited when my mother came home. I remember moving to live with her in Maryland once she purchased our home. I remember how painful it was to grow up without her. Thinking back, I was too young to comprehend what was going on. As an adult, I can say that I was blessed to grow up in a loving home with Grandma and Pop, who made sure I lived a normal, happy life in my mother's absence. Growing up, every kid had someone they looked up to, whether it be an athlete or a superhero; mine was my mother. Even in her physical absence through my ups and downs, she had always been there for me, my biggest supporter and guidance counselor.

My mother is not only a role model to me; she also has thousands of students whose lives she has touched and changed. My mother is an amazing woman, always being her true authentic self. She is welcoming with open arms and has one of the biggest hearts I know. My mother lives a life that gives people hope. She has been through so many challenges and pitfalls in her life, yet she never gave up. Her life is a living testament to what perseverance can do. Through it all, she overcame every adversity in her path. Dr. Glenn is not only a phenomenal woman, leader, educator, daughter, sister, aunt, family member, friend, sorority sister, and game changer; she is my mother and my hero. I pray this book touches, inspires, and motivates all who read it. May your lives be blessed with the message that it gives.

Andrew McCurvin, Jr.

Table of Contents

Chapter 1: A Dream Deferred   1

Chapter 2: Broken   8

Chapter 3: Reality Check   16

Chapter 4: Sentencing   19

Chapter 5: Alderson   26

Chapter 6: Summer 1991   31

Chapter 7: Drug House   39

Chapter 8: Trapped in a Weaved Web   41

Chapter 9: Danbury   49

Chapter 10: The Transition   55

Chapter 11: Pre-judgement   60

Chapter 12: Against All Odds   61

Chapter 13: The Earthquake   64

Chapter 14: Ongoing Challenges   70

Chapter 15: Being a Parent   72

Chapter 16: Writing Retreat   74

Chapter 17: Not Every Caterpillar Turns Into a Butterfly   79

About the Author   84

Chapter 1:

A Dream Deferred

The day was finally here—my graduation from The College of William and Mary. The last discussion that my dad and I had before his passing was getting into a doctorate program. Here I was—three and a half years from beginning to end, and I'd made it. Finally, my life-long dream was coming to fruition.

My name was called. I walked proudly across the front to receive my degree. As I shook hands with the right hand and grabbed my degree with my left, my mind was spinning, thinking back to the day the cell door slammed, and how I thought this moment would never happen.

I grew up in inner-city Connecticut. Although I saw a lot, I stayed on a straight and narrow path. My mother sacrificed to send me to Catholic schools from fourth through twelfth grade to escape all possible distractions. I grew up knowing I was going to be a pediatrician. It seemed like yesterday that I was a student on the campus of Virginia State University, striving to be a pediatrician. My heart was set on becoming a doctor. I can admit my grades were not top-notch, nor was

I was in the top ten percent of my class, but so what? I still had a dream, and moving in the direction of getting there was the first step. I only applied to two universities: Howard University in Washington, D.C., and Virginia State University in Petersburg, VA. I was not accepted to Howard. I guess my grades were not good enough, but I did not care. All I could think about was all my family in that area who might pop up while I was enjoying college life.

The moment I received my acceptance letter from Virginia State University (VSU), I was ecstatic. My cousin, Frances, and I were going together. I responded immediately, and of course, we both requested each other as roommates. The school year couldn't end soon enough. I was going off to an HBCU (Historically Black College/University) to pursue my lifelong dream. I remember that day so vividly; our family had charted a bus to our family reunion in Jacksonville, NC. Frances and I got off with our bags into a cousin's car to be dropped off on campus for our freshman orientation.

Many of us young teenagers soon-to-be-young-adults were off on our own away from parental guidance and rules. Now was the time for us to use what was instilled in us for the past eighteen years of teaching and training from our parents; in my case, my single mom. Howard Hall was my dorm assignment, room 418. There were two beds, two desks, and two wardrobes. To us, it was our first apartment with a public bathroom down the hall. How was this going to work? Did we have to set up shower schedules? Not to mention one payphone on each side of the hall for a hall full of girls. I could not imagine waiting in a line to call home. One phone was probably going to be the worst part of college life.

Those thoughts were short-lived after all the excitement of moving in and meeting our hall-mates. There was no greater feeling than connecting with people from all over the United States. Some of us stayed connected after graduation while others got caught up in life and stayed away. I, too, got caught up in life. My journey to hell and back brought me to a place where I was accepted with open arms by some, and by others, it was a case of everybody was watching. *How dare you shame the family with your actions?* When I say actions, I mean my falling in love with a drug dealer. *You weren't raised like that. How could you?* Already feeling the weight of life on my shoulders, I didn't need the "I told you so" speech. I needed to hear "It's over; you made it through. Now let's work on getting you back on your feet."

I guess I understood the anger and disappointment to a certain degree, but I was broken already. I needed my loved ones to help build me back up. What I thought I needed then wasn't what I needed at all. I had to realize that it wasn't about them. It wasn't about anyone; it was about me. How was I going to handle this roadblock to redemption while building a life with my son? He was two years old when I left. I remember staring at him all night before the verdict. It's like God was preparing me for the inevitable. Was that night the last time I would hold him, tell him I loved him for a long time?

Chapter 2:

Broken

I knew a guilty verdict was coming my way. Once all those thoughts flooded my mind, I began questioning myself. Could I survive without him? He was my everything, and I was his. I kept my thoughts to myself. I by no means wanted to say to my mother, "I am going to prison." After all, this is the same woman who told me over three years ago that "When you go to jail, I'm not coming to see you." I remember that day as if it were yesterday. What did she know? I wasn't going to jail. Why would I? What did his actions have to do with me? Those thoughts played over and over in my mind. As I stood up in court to hear the verdict, "Guilty," my heart dropped with the idea of leaving my son alone, motherless.

I felt an onset of mixed emotions—at one point, numbness. Guilty on three counts. The only thing I was guilty of was loving a man that did not love me. My heart was saddened at the thought of leaving my son behind. Yet, I was all too grateful to get out of the prison I was already in—my marriage. Overwhelmed, I began to cry. I was handcuffed, shackled, and taken to Westchester County Jail in Valhalla, New York.

Westchester County Jail was full of petty thieves and drug addicts; one-woman cells with a bed and toilet. Now, this was jail like you saw on television. Except that the doors slid shut. No bars, but no privacy with a window.

My first days were odd on a cell block all day, no recreation as the television often portrayed. However, there were classes we could take to leave the cellblock. There was a hair class where you could get your hair done, a computer class to learn computer skills, and a self-esteem class to seek the root of your choices. I attended all three classes over the fifteen months that I was there. The self-esteem course was the most powerful and life-changing class for me. We were given journals to write in; nothing was openly discussed if we did not want to, but we could write everything we were feeling down.

The counselor wanted us to dig deep and tap into our emotions. We talked about different topics. One of the topics was child abuse—all types of abuse, such as physical, mental, emotional, and sexual abuse.

The counselor asked, "Do you ever recall a time when you may have been the victim of abuse?" Initially, I could not remember a time when I was abused, but as I began to dig deeper, my memory resurfaced, and I began to cry. As a child between the ages of five and nine, a family member molested me. That was the most horrific and traumatic experience as a child. So painful and traumatic that I buried it away. After all, who would want to remember being violated? I was twenty-seven years old now, in jail at the time of this revelation.

I grew up in an abusive household. I remember an incident when my dad broke into the house. Being scared as a little girl, I ran downstairs to the neighbors to call the police. Another experience that repeatedly played in my head was being called a bitch by my mother's boyfriend. My mother made me apologize to him to keep the house's peace. So as I reminisce about these incidents in my life, I realize I was broken from the beginning. Molested by a cousin and disrespected by a man, being forced to wallow in that shit, a broken little girl became a broken and abused woman—whose way out of an abusive marriage was prison.

When my mother told me she was not coming to see me when I went to jail, my response was, "I am not going to jail. I have done nothing." I knew nothing about the Ricco laws; having knowledge of the crime was the same as a person committing the crime.

Another conversation I had with my mother was when she told me I married my father. I looked at her puzzled; it took a minute for that to sink in. As I was sitting in my jail cell, it clicked. Something I never thought about; I married an abusive man that sold drugs. She was right again.

For a daughter, our father is our first love, and you look for that in the men you date; attentive and generous, but no affection. I did not grow up with affection in my home. I knew my mother loved me, and my dad loved me, but there were no hugs and no kisses, and no "I love you." When I had Drew, I kissed him, hugged him, and rubbed his little ears. I read to him and loved him the way I wish I had been loved. My mother was young, abused, and did the best she could. I did blame her back then. I was angry as a little girl but could not find the words to express what I felt. During my childhood, I was raised to believe that children were seen, not heard; thus, my feelings were suppressed. When I did speak, I lashed out and got popped in the mouth. As a youngster, I stayed on punishment. I was angry all the time but did not know why.

I see the same anger in my young elementary school students. I see the same emotions in my middle school students—angry with low self-esteem. It is mind-blowing how years of suppression and abuse can affect your adult life, especially relationships. I have not been in a healthy relationship for most of my adult life.

Years later, when I got to Alderson West Virginia Federal Prison Camp, the abuse became openly expressed at a revival. I can't remember who the evangelist was, but when I say she broke through barriers and chains, I mean it.

This woman of GOD said, "You are here because you made a choice that you don't fully understand; let me break it down for you. Let's go back to your childhood. I need everyone to close your eyes. If you were raped as a child, I need you to stand up."

My husband raped me, so I didn't stand.

"You choose these types of men," she said, and then described the types of men that rape victims chose. She went through all types of abuses and described the types of men these women chose in their adult lives. The evangelist then said, "If you were ever molested as a child, stand." My heart dropped, yes I recalled the incident as if it was yesterday, but now I was asked to stand so people would see me. I was a child, and I was violated, and as an adult, I stood there full of shame. This was the first time I had publicly acknowledged this horrible act. It was one thing to write about the abuse, but now I had to publicly stand and face it.

She then went on to characterize my ex-husband as if she knew him personally. I cried even harder. I heard her say, "Open your eyes." As I looked around, every woman in the room was standing and crying.

The tragedies of my childhood shaped my mind and life in the direction of self-destruction. I had placed my self-worth and lack of self-confidence in the hands of a man that didn't give a damn about me, but why would he? I didn't. Not only do victims take on shame, they feel guilty too, as if we could have stopped it. From my early childhood, I had learned to keep quiet and suppress those things that hurt me. Suppression can turn into health issues. I had developed high blood pressure by the time I was thirty-five years old.

All my life, I had been chubby. My dad's nickname for me was Tubby Glenn. Holding on to weight has everything to do with emotions, stress, and, of course, poor eating habits. The mind is so powerful. The underlying issues of such surrounded me in that revival—women that were broken, bound, and in prison within themselves and their relationships before even coming to prison. We were from different backgrounds, yet we had so much in common and ended up in the same place.

When that revelation came back to me in Westchester County, the counselor then said, "If it's still too painful to talk about, write it in a letter. Address it to whomever you choose to tell even if you have no intentions of mailing it, at least you let it out."

I wrote a letter to my mother, never to be sent. When I got transferred, the box with my property was mailed to my home address. The letter was in the box; that's how my mother found out. We talked about it later, and I told her who it was. She got quiet. At that point, I think she blamed herself. I let her know it wasn't her fault or mine.

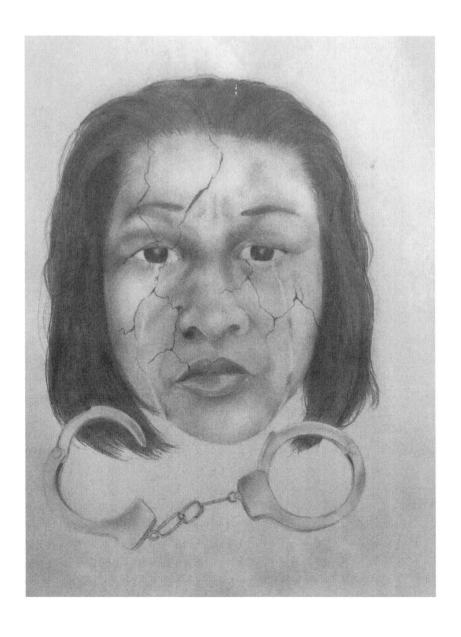

DR. ANTOINETTE M. GLENN

Chapter 3:
Reality Check

I married a percentage of my father. My ex-husband did not love me unconditionally. I often wonder if he ever loved me at all. How could he when the feds offered him a deal to plead out, and I would not do any time, and he refused? A man who was undoubtedly guilty, yet he was still willing to sacrifice my freedom, leaving our son alone on the outside without parents. What a massive lesson to learn—a man, your husband, wanting you to go down with him just to give him a sense of still being in control of your life. As I moved from facility to facility because he was my husband, he located me. When I was released and moved to Maryland, he could still find me even after the divorce in the early 2000s. Public records led him to me when I bought my house. He was able to contact me by mail, a never-ending nightmare.

By then, I was over the fear, and he no longer had control of anything, not even when he had to lock down in prison. Drew would communicate with his father and his siblings on Facebook, letters, pictures, and phone calls until he asked his father that nagging question that troubled him growing up. Why didn't you do anything to help my mom?

My ex-husband responded with, "She was benefiting from what I was doing." That response locked Drew's heart of ever having a relationship with him.

Drew told him, "My mother never said anything negative to me about you; she never stopped me from communicating with you. All I have is my mom and my grandmother, and they are the only people I trust. I don't know you, nor do I want to at this point."

My self-esteem was low when I met my ex-husband. I was a college graduate and couldn't find a job. It became worse when I married him. He made me feel inferior like I was incapable of making decisions. He often reminded me that his baby mothers with no degrees had jobs, and I had one and couldn't get one. He took control of every aspect of our lives. During that time, my confidence was lost. His behavior carried a broad spectrum of intimidation.

A threat he'd often said was, "If you don't listen, you will feel." His tactic was manipulation and physical abuse. I was in a prison of control.

We, as a people, believe criticism more than we believe praise. One cruel statement has much more impact than one hundred positive ones. While in prison, thoughts about my future ran through my mind. I made a pact with myself that I would never live by man's limitations. There was so much that I had to offer that I refused to stop until I was where I wanted to be in life.

My biggest challenge in life was my incarceration, but it has proven to be my greatest teacher. I learned more during that time than I had my entire life. I learned about people from different walks of life. Things I never experienced personally, I saw doing time. Addicts on heroin achy and needing methadone to take the edge off; pregnant women taking AZT so their unborn children wouldn't contract HIV. Westchester county was a revolving door. I was there for fifteen months, and the same women were released and would return all during my time there. I realized that addiction was a severe disease. They had no control, and their support system didn't exist. Yet, I was here with them as a support system, but just the same, I was an inmate doing time.

Chapter 4:

Sentencing

When I was initially sentenced, I was sentenced to ninety-seven months with five years of supervised release. The federal government does not have probation; you get fifty-four days off a year for good time. I was charged with three counts. Count one: Conspiracy to possess with intent to distribute. Count thirteen: Possession with intent to distribute cocaine and cocaine base, which, according to the sentencing guidelines rendered me a base offense level of thirty-four, then the feds added two points to the base because they claimed my participation in my husband's drug operation was supervisory. Count Twenty-nine: Money laundering base was twenty because there was only $27,800 in the safety deposit box; three points were added because the proceeds were unlawful. After going back and reading the paperwork, little did I know that count one maximum prison term was life, count nineteen mandatory minimum was ten years of imprisonment, and count twenty-nine maximum term of imprisonment was twenty years.

Wow. There I was, a young black woman in her late twenties, with her whole life ahead of her, yet I was facing 188-235 months in prison based on the offense level of thirty-six with no prior criminal history. Let's break that down to years: I was facing up to twenty years as a college graduate and mother of a two-year-old with no priors.

At trial, the federal agents mentioned that during one of their surveillances in New York, my physical attack was so bad that they were going to stop the surveillance so they could stop my ex-husband from hitting me. Imagine seeing it, knowing it to be fact, yet they were willing to sentence my life away? Hearing that in court and knowing they saw it and did nothing was a heavy pill to swallow.

Thinking back to that incident, one of many, I try so hard to forget. I had gotten into an argument with him, so he hauled off and started punching me. I wanted to jump out of the car as he was driving, but on a busy New York street, I could have been killed, and the thought of leaving my son with him was not an option. I would take the punches to have the ability to hold him again.

I was going to prison, and as ironic as it had seemed, a part of me was relieved. I was finally getting away from my ex-husband. At sentencing back in 1996, I stood up and said that I felt free for the first time in a long time, free from that abusive, volatile marriage. At one point, I wanted out so bad that I considered committing suicide to get away from him. Thank God, my king inside me was three months along, and I could feel butterflies, so I did not. Drew saved our lives. I never shared that with him. He is destined for greatness. His purpose was to save me. Knowing I had him kept me motivated. Prison gave me time to find and rebuild myself back to a functioning, healthy, emotional, and mental wellbeing.

I developed a love for lifting weights and running while in prison. I felt good. The heaviness was lifted. Over the years, I have struggled with my weight, still carrying my past baggage with me. On the outside looking in, you'd see a happy, always smiling woman; but on the inside, there was emotional turmoil. Even after being released and moving to Maryland, I still hadn't released the baggage I was carrying. Even after securing a job with the school system, walking into the dealership and purchasing my first car, and a few months later closing on the home that I paid for all by myself. For many, that would read success, but that little, broken girl inside me was still hurting, and the broken woman she had become was stuck in time.

I was in Cranston Adult Correctional Facility in Cranston, Rhode Island at the time of sentencing. I was found guilty on January 18, 1995, and sentenced to ninety-seven months on March 29, 1996. I was now federal inmate #11536-014.

At sentencing, I stood up and said, "One day, I will write a book, hoping that I will reach out to the many women who are or may find themselves in the same situation."

However, while the sentencing guidelines say an offense with a level of thirty-six requires mandatory imprisonment 188 to 235 months, Judge C showed leniency. He reduced my points. Two for coercion and duress; my participation was due to my abusive husband. I can't remember what other points were taken off, but God's grace gave this judge empathy for a lost, broken soul. I will always appreciate him for that.

The feds were angry that I didn't plead out and didn't testify against my ex. After all that he did to me, I was still in love and under his control. Testifying was not an option, nor was I going to make a deal. I told them they had all they needed—the undercover agent he sold to, the CI's, and the twenty plus co-defendants that all signed statements.

"You have a young son. We will offer you ten years instead of the twenty you are facing if you plead out."

I replied, "I'll take my chances."

They were pissed, and my lawyer all but told me so. When you plead guilty, there's no coming back later and asking for an appeal or consideration to vacate sentence; so off to trial I went. Ten years was 120 months; when I received my ninety-seven months, I was relieved. It worked out for the best. As a result, I could go back and appeal. Eight years meant I'd be home while my son was in elementary school and middle school, and I'd still have time to raise him.

Once I got to my destination, I was going to start my appeal process. I mentioned it to my attorney, but he said ninety-seven months was a lot better, and it could have been worse. I didn't like the response; I just knew I did not want to do eight years away from my now three-year-old son. I left when he was two, thinking that by the time I was sentenced,

I'd get time served, and we'd be back together. Since that was not the case, I was determined to file an appeal more than ever and get my sentence reduced. Yes, ninety-seven months was not 120 months, but it was still too much time.

Before sentencing, you are held in county jails and other holding facilities. You do not enter the Bureau of Prisons until after you are sentenced. When I was first found guilty, I was taken to Westchester County in Valhalla, New York. I did fifteen months, and from there I was taken to Cranston Adult Correctional facility in Cranston, Rhode Island until sentencing.

Once I was sentenced, the U.S. Marshals picked me up and took me to an airport. I was unsure of which one, but I was almost certain it was a military one. Sharpshooters surrounded the plane. You'd think we were in a movie with all the Marshalls and prisoners awaiting direction to move forward to board the aircraft, the sharpshooters ready to take you out with any sudden movement.

There were more men than women, of course, so they put the men on first. They were the most significant threat. It wasn't like they had one-to-one ratio manpower to control us all, but they had the hardware to scare us into not doing anything stupid. As we stood on one side, the guys were put on the other side. They stared at us like we were pieces of meat. It's only natural, looking back, but believe me, I was not interested in getting a pen pal. Once the guys were put on, we went next. *Shackles on my feet*, why was that song playing in my head? That was not the time for that.

As much as I liked that song, never in a million years would I think I'd be in shackles, handcuffed with a chain connecting the two; we had to walk like penguins as to not fall on our faces. The old school song by Frank James, "Shackles on my feet won't let me move ... take off these shackles," played in my head. Years later, Mary Mary's song "Shackles" came along, talking about trials. Both songs convey the same message: surviving trials, so now it's time to dance and show praise. Sometimes your blessings come from unconventional places. God uses people to show you that he is in control of every situation.

As we entered the plane, the Marshalls were everywhere, one standing straight ahead, issuing us to come forward and pointing to where he wanted us to sit. As I walked on the plane, the guys were turning and watching. The ones on the aisle seat were able to touch us slyly; one touched my butt as I passed. If I could spit fire, he'd be burnt. Once I made it to my seat, I felt so much better. I had a window seat, so I put the shade down; not even a minute later, the Marshall told me to raise it, so I put it back up halfway after all that sun was beaming in my face. He returned and said, "All the way up." I sighed and put it up. What, did he think I was sending a signal to my getaway car with all the security I just saw? *Please get me to where we are going, it's been a long day, and it's nowhere near over.*

When we got in the air, we were told we were going to Oklahoma. *Oklahoma, what in the world is there?* I thought to myself. That's a state I never thought about, yet I was on a plane full of Marshalls and felons, and away we went. As I later found out, Oklahoma was the Bureau of

Prisons control center. It's like the nucleus in the cell that controls and regulates the activities of the cell. The BOP controls and regulates where the prisoners were going. Here I was referencing the cell after spending fifteen months in a cell in Westchester County.

In Westchester County, we could come in and out most of the day, but we had to lock down during the shift change to be counted and at night to go to sleep. I was so excited to get to Oklahoma because here was where they would tell me I was going to Danbury, a Federal Prison thirty-five minutes from home. I'd be able to see Drew weekly. To my disappointment, I was told I was going to Alderson, West Virginia; my request to be closer to home was not considered. The government isn't for helping families stay together. Prison is modern-day slavery, shipping us far away to break ties and to break us down even more. My heart was crushed, and my spirits sunk even lower. I had to call and tell my family the bad news. Where the hell is West Virginia? Is that next to Virginia on the west side? I wasn't good at geography. First chance I got, I was going to look it up on the map. Now I had two things to do when I got to my destination—get this appeal started and find out how far West Virginia was from Waterbury, Connecticut.

Chapter 5:

Alderson

Once you were told where you were going, it was a waiting game until that day came. When it was your time to go, you were woken early and told to get ready to fly out. Here I went again, shackles and all—but at least this time I was going to my destination. I got to Alderson, West Virginia, and it was beautiful. It reminded me of a college campus. I was assigned to my cottage (in college, it would be called a dormitory; this felt like Déjá vu). I was given keys to my door, and I walked in; there were two bunk beds, two desks, two hutches, one on either side of the room. If you had to do time, you'd want to be in a place like this, not an overcrowded state facility.

Niantic, the women's state facility at that time of my arrest, was overcrowded; we had to sleep on mattresses on the dining hall floor. You were given toiletries and had to change into a prison uniform; that was a scared straight moment, my heart dropped. I wasn't a small chick, always thick, so I wasn't worried about being raped (movies); nonetheless, I had already decided that I wasn't going in the showers and only going to the restroom when we went in groups. I called my mother to let her know I was okay. As I talked to my mom, a woman was on the next phone with her loved ones, telling them she and her husband were no longer together; she was now with Mikey. Mikey was a bearded woman standing next to her. I felt like I was in the Twilight Zone with no exit door; that weekend felt like hell.

On Monday, I was arraigned and released to my mother's house where I would await trial; little did I know that trial would come almost two years later. Meanwhile, I went on with my life, got a job; life felt almost normal again. My ex-husband was a flight risk, so he was detained. He'd come to the U.S. from Jamaica on a full track and field scholarship to Texas A&M University. He went AWOL after meeting up with his brother in the Bronx. His brother introduced him to the drug world.

My ex-husband grew up poor with his mom and siblings. He was fascinated with the fast money and his ability to live a life he could only dream of back in Jamaica. He soon found out that there were no friends in the drug world. His brother was murdered in front of him by a man he considered his friend. You see, in the drug world, your friends become your enemies when you start making more money and driving better cars. There are only two ways out: death or prison. Unfortunately, death and prison were usually the result of someone you knew. Too bad my ex-husband didn't remember this same lesson years later. The 1991 movie *New Jack City* was reality at its best. My ex-husband was introduced to the undercover agent by a friend who was later identified as a Confidential Informant (CI). He met up with a yardy (that's what they call fellow Jamaicans) and started his drug trade in Connecticut once his brother was killed. The moment a woman took him in, he no longer traveled back and forth from New York.

Chapter 6:

Summer 1991

I came home after graduating from VSU in the summer of 1991. I didn't want to live in Connecticut, so my aunt said I could come to Maryland and look for a job there. At that time, AIDS was running rampant, and I wanted to get a job in a lab, possibly the National Institute of Health (NIH), to do some research. Going straight off to medical school was not an option; I'd have to do some significant work to get my portfolio and transcripts where they needed to be. Partying and not being fully focused on academics, I graduated with a 2.3 GPA. I was not too fond of chemistry, but I had to take it as a pre-med major. NIH and other government agencies were an option. If I could get into one of them, maybe I could help find a cure for this virus that killed so many people. Unlike bacteria, viruses mutate, so it's almost impossible to find a cure for something that is continuously changing. The labs didn't pan out, and my self-esteem wasn't at its best. Here I was, a college graduate, and I couldn't find a job. *Oh well, let me go home and hang out for the summer and try again in August.*

In July 1991, I met my ex-husband outside my girlfriend's house; my mom had made her some banana pudding, and I went by to drop it off. When I got out of the car, that's when he saw me. I'd just gotten in from D.C., I had a new asymmetrical cut, my nails were done, and my legs were out. He was in a car parked in front of her house; he asked her my name and introduced himself.

That evening, I came back through after hanging out, and again he was parked in front of her house. *What, is this dude stalking me?* I thought. I was a fresh face, a thick body, and a college graduate. His approach couldn't be the same as it had been for the neighborhood girls. He asked if he could take me out. I hesitated, then I told him I was only home for the summer, not interested. We began talking, and I gave him my number; no cell phones back then. He called me the next day and asked if he could take me out for ice cream. From that day forward, he'd come by and take me out. I thought it was just something to do until I headed back to Maryland. I started liking this guy; he was charming, very attentive, and I was falling for the Okie Doke. I left, went back to Maryland with the same results. I was frustrated with the job search. My car registration was about to be suspended because of a speeding ticket. I headed back to Connecticut to take care of my registration and never returned to Maryland.

By the end of 1991, my ex-husband and I moved in together. My mother saw the transformation right before her eyes. One day she asked me to look at myself in the mirror.

"Do you even know the person staring back at you?"

I said, "Yes," as I thought, *What kind of question is that?*

She then went on to say, "When you go to prison, I am not coming to visit you."

I gave her this puzzled stare. "What are you talking about? I'm not doing anything to go to prison."

"Well, he is," she said. "I looked him up, and he has a prior drug charge. So that's where you are headed dealing with him."

I was hot as fish grease. How dare she say I'm going to prison? Not even two years later, 5.am. on July 13, 1993, DEA, ATF, and other federal agents knocked down the door. I had just finished feeding Drew.

As I got back in bed, I could hear doors slamming. My ex-husband said to look out the window and see if anyone was messing with the car. As I looked, the agents were storming up the stairs with guns pointed. There I stood, frozen, naked, with guns aimed at both him and me. In the next room, I could hear Drew crying. My heart dropped; the agents would not let me move to get him. They wanted to know if there were guns or drugs in the house. My ex-husband let them know there were guns under the bed. The women officer went into the closet and gave me a shirt, a pair of jeans, no panties or bra, but a pair of sneakers. One of the agents holding Drew told me to call my mother to come to get him. He then told me my mother's name, address, and telephone number. I was startled. How did he know that? We later found out my ex-husband had been under surveillance for the past six months, and his portable phone and our house phone was taped.

I was distraught. I called my mom and asked her to please come to get Drew. "The feds have busted down the door."

She said, "Feds? What is going on? I am on my way." Imagine that call. She'd told me this was going to happen and I didn't listen. Before she got there, we were whisked away down to the precinct. Twenty-five people were arrested that day. The newspaper headlines read "Jamaican Drug Kingpin and Wife" ran for weeks. It felt like I was in a nightmare, one that I wouldn't wake up from; my whole life flashed before me.

I graduated on Mother's Day, May 1991, met my ex-husband in July 1991, and married him on my birthday in February 1992, at the Justice of the Peace. On December 9, 1992, I gave birth to Drew (on his father's birthday); in March 1993, I went to Jamaica to meet his family. My ex-husband flew using a fake passport. He paid my cousin's boyfriend to use his birth certificate and social security card. The feds met up with the boyfriend to question him about the passport. He then told the feds about the deal he had made with my ex-husband and that my ex-husband was a drug dealer. The trip to Jamaica served two purposes: to visit family and take all the money in the safe. I wonder if my ex-husband knew he was under investigation and blew it off like everything else. I remember being with my ex-husband when he met up with the undercover agent, his new friend. I am not street smart, but I knew you shouldn't allow strangers into your life. I asked him about this new friend. He told me to mind my business.

When my mother picked my son up, she asked the agents if they had a search warrant. They lied and told her they gave it to us; we never saw one, nor did they mention having one. When I got downtown to the police station, I saw a familiar face and told him to contact my dad.

The police officer said, "Antoinette Glenn, are you related to Clarence Glenn, street name Scatch?"

I said "Yes, that's my father." He said, "Like father like daughter, huh?" My dad was a drug dealer. Not all my life, but he never brought drugs around me throughout my teenage years to adulthood. My dad owned tractor trailers. He would drive for multiple companies up and down the east coast. My friends would come to find me in class and tell me my dad was there. I'd get back to the dorm, and there he was with this big eighteen-wheeler in Howard Hall's parking lot. He would stop by on his way back from Florida to drop us off some grapefruits and oranges.

During the summers, my dad would get loads of watermelons from the South and sell them off his refrigerated truck. Those watermelons were some kind of good. My dad had a high school diploma but never went to college. Instead, he enlisted in the Marines after high school. He did four years and came out. He was a carpenter and real estate investor. He would take an abandoned house and make it look brand new, a man of many trades. My dad was raised by his father and his stepmother, who we called Mama. It wasn't until I got older that I found out my biological grandmother left her three children with my grandfather and went off to remarry and have another set of children in Ohio.

A little boy abandoned by his mother, no wonder my dad's respect for women wasn't high. My mother was the only woman he married. Remember that song by the Temptations, "Papa was a rolling stone, wherever he laid his hat was his home?" My dad loved women, and whomever he was dating, he'd treat her children just like his own. Although he only had five biological sons and three biological daughters (the eldest daughter was adopted by her mother's husband), he'd claim an additional five boys and three girls. As my dad got older, his health began to deteriorate. He was found dead in his apartment one day. With so many health issues, no autopsy was warranted. My brother, Calvin, spoke to my dad every day, and when he couldn't get in touch with him, he called me to see if I had spoken to him. I hadn't since earlier that week. He then called Connecticut and had someone go by and check on him. The building supervisor went into the apartment, and there he was on the floor in the living room dead. His cellphone was in the bedroom.

When I received the call, it was my brother. I thought maybe he'd talked to Dad. I answered the phone, and he was crying. "Nette, Dad is dead." The moment my brother told me, my body went numb. I didn't hear anything after that. I told my assistant principal and gathered up my things to leave. As I walked past the office, my principal asked me where I was going. I told him my dad had died, and I was going to Connecticut.

He said, "I am so sorry to hear that; take as much time as you need." As I walked out of the building, I felt numb, too numb to cry. All I knew was my first love, the man that cherished the ground I walked on, was gone. Our last conversation had been a week prior. When did I plan to get into a Doctorate program, and was a convertible Mercedes still my favorite car? The answer was always "once I find the right fit," and "yes, I still like the convertible Mercedes."

My father came to my high school graduation, but he didn't come to my VSU graduation (he was in prison). But when I graduated from Coppin State University with my Master's degree, he was there, front and center. He was a proud dad; with all that he had done in his life, I was his pride and joy. I had gone to prison and came out and continued striving toward my goals. In May 2019, when I received my Doctorate from the College of William & Mary, it was a bittersweet day. How proud he would be to see his girl walk and receive the Doctorate degree. I dedicated my dissertation to both my dad and Drew, the two men in my life that love me unconditionally.

I turned and looked up at the sky and said, "I did it, Dad," as tears flowed down my face. I survived a death sentence of a marriage, did five years three months, two days, eight hours, and four minutes in federal prison, and that day I reached another milestone in my life. My perseverance and determination beat the odds, and I did it.

Chapter 7:

Drug House

My ex-husband had a drug house across town where he did most, if not all, of his transactions; the undercover agent was aware of this information.

The night before the big bust, my ex-husband said, "I have to go to New York; let's go."

I did not want to go but talking back or refusing could result in getting hit; so off we went. The first time he hit me, I remember him saying, "If you don't listen, you will feel." It totally caught me off guard because no man had ever hit me, not even my father, until that day.

We went to New York, and less than eight hours later, the feds were busting down the door. I didn't know that the undercover agent had requested a certain amount that he needed early that next morning; he wanted to make sure the drugs were in the house and not across town in the drug house. My ex-husband looked at me and said, "J.J.," his newfound friend. I was a college graduate with no priors, and the mother of a seven-month-old when we were first arrested, and none of that mattered. My affiliation with the crime was being married to the man committing the crime. I depended on him for everything; it became second nature.

Chapter 8:

Trapped in a Weaved Web

Whenever I needed to get things for Drew, he'd say, "On your way out, such and such is going to meet you. Give him this and get what you need with the money he gives you." I never considered myself a drug dealer. Was I? Before I knew it, I became entangled in his mess. As our relationship progressed, my values were diminished. Who was this woman staring back at me in the mirror? I didn't know, and I didn't like her. His control over me was indescribable. I was desperately in love with him and afraid of him at the same time. I was in a city full of family, yet I was so secluded from them. I felt like I was in a foreign country. My relationship with my mother slowly deteriorated to the extent that we stopped talking.

We were both arrested and taken into custody. The condo was in my name (possession), conspiracy to distribute, and money laundering (safety deposit box). After getting robbed a year before, my ex-husband had me get a safety deposit box; little did I know I would get charged with money laundering a year later.

We got into an argument in April 1992 and he struck me with a solid wood frame. I became dizzy. I was pregnant with Drew and fighting a man—not just any man, but my husband. My eye caught sight of a straight razor on the dresser. I grabbed it and started swinging it toward him. I cut him—where, I didn't know—but I was able to get away. I must have jumped down the stairs because I was out of the front door in the car before I knew it. I was full of fear, and my unborn baby was feeling all of this misery. I drove myself to the hospital to make sure everything was okay. I had a cartoon knot on my forehead and a mild concussion, but Drew was unharmed. Feeling ashamed, I didn't call my mom. I stayed home that night, scared to death that he was going to come kill me. He called and checked on me and told me he would never hit me again. He came home, but as sure as the sky was blue, he told me he'd kill me if I ever fought him again. I believed him.

Womanizer was an understatement. My ex-husband had women in every city, baby mommas, you name it. They'd call the house, the pager, and the portable phone all hours of the day and night. We'd argue, but I never defended myself after the threat of killing me, not even when he raped me. No is no, husband or not, but to him, he owned me. He did.

The female officer at the precinct was singing, "bad boys, bad boys, what you going to do what you going to do when they come for you." I was hot as fish grease. This was not a joke. I started seeing other co-defendants come into the station. I didn't know them, but I was sure they knew me, all but one pled out, and the others signed statements against my ex-husband and some against me; the few times my ex-husband had a few meet me was enough to get me entangled in the web that was being weaved.

Behind closed doors, I was sleeping with the enemy. I felt like there was no way out until the day I was found guilty; it was death or prison for me. I was set free from my prison of a marriage to the Bureau of Prisons. I was finally free. Even if it meant leaving my baby to be raised by my mother, at least I was alive.

My mind was at ease, knowing that Drew would be loved and taken care of in my absence. It broke my heart to know his heart would be broken. He was my world, and I was his. We read books. He knew his ABCs by the time he was two and could identify them. I loved him so much, and now I was leaving him and had no idea when I would return. My mom brought him to see me twice while I was in Alderson, West Virginia. He came for Thanksgiving and Field Day. I saw him twice in three years. That was painful, but at least I'd speak to him often. We'd both be so excited to hear each other's voices. We would sing "I love you, and you love me." That was our Anthem during his Barney phase.

I worked in the kitchen in both prisons as a cook. Alderson had a population of over two hundred women, and Danbury had a little over half. Everyone had to work to pay the assessment fee's restitution and to have money to get necessities. It was a full workday; there was no lying around.

All my thoughts were focused on staying positive and reclaiming my sense of self. I needed to find Antoinette again. I had a son that needed me, and I needed him. I began working on my appeal when I got to Alderson. I knew nothing about the law, but it didn't take a rocket scientist to know that how I was charged was unfair. The crack laws were meant to affect the African American population. The children were collateral damage, being raised by family or put in the foster care system. I was not a lawyer, but I knew how to read and knew how to write. I spent a lot of time in the library looking up cases. I had to research case law that would overturn the decision of charging me as an equal to my ex-husband. I contacted my attorney and told him I wanted to file an appeal.

He said, "Appeal? What? You were facing twenty years and only received eight years." In essence, he was saying I should be happy with what I was given. I had to remember he was court-appointed; it's not like I was paying him big bucks to stop at nothing to get me out.

I was disappointed but still determined. My ex-husband controlled my life, and I vowed never to let anyone else do it. I came across something called 2255, which had to do with ineffective counsel. I had discrepancies even Stevie Wonder could see. I wrote the court and asked them to send me a copy of all the transcripts. I had nothing but time to go through them like a fine-tooth comb, and that I did.

Ground one of my appeal: The district court erred in calculating the base offense level regarding my conduct. At the time of the surveillance, my ex-husband sold between twenty to fifty kilos. As I read, I began to scratch my head; the feds put that on me too. The Presentencing Investigation report PSI was a document I should have received at least ten days before sentencing, yet my first time seeing it was the morning of sentencing. My due process was violated. There was no evidentiary hearing. Maybe there was, but I knew nothing about it and definitely would have opposed the findings related to my involvement. Again, he was pro bono.

I contacted the courts again and asked for another attorney. The court wrote back and indicated my appointed attorney would have to submit. I wrote a letter to my attorney requesting an appeal. I even put in the letter what needed to be appealed—the base offense level of thirty-four. Staying diligent and consistent was my aim. My son was four years old, and he needed me. Again, I went to the library and constructed a motion to modify the sentence to the U.S. District Court. My verbiage and legal jargon would make one think I was an attorney—well, at least a paralegal. I wrote my appeal; all I needed was an attorney to submit it to the U.S Court of Appeals.

On December 5, 1997, my appeal went before the Appellate Court. I won. I received a sentence reduction from ninety-seven months to seventy-eight months. My eight years one month was now six years and six months. I was already down for over two years. It was a victory, but I wanted time served. I was the little engine that could. I didn't get furloughed to go back to the court. My mother and Ms. Brown, her long-time friend, attended court that day in my absence. I could only imagine my mother's face when she heard that my sentence would be reduced. I later received the paperwork that stated affirmed in part and remanded in part for resentencing. Now it was time for me to transfer closer to home. With a year left, I could see Drew weekly, and my family could visit regularly. Finally, I was on the downside. The light was peeking through at the end of my tunnel.

I went to the warden and asked to be transferred back to Connecticut. My transfer was granted. Asking and pursuing was a habit that I had become accustomed to. Although my sentence was reduced to seventy-eight months, I still felt that it was too harsh. I filed a motion to receive a copy of the transcripts from the resentencing hearing held on December 5, 1997. I also filed a motion to modify my reduced sentence in November 1998. Both were denied. The three grounds that I needed addressed were:

Ground One: The District Court erred in calculating the base offense level regarding my relevant conduct. In accordance with the United States Court of Appeals 2nd Circuit's summary order, I objected to the base offense level of thirty-four, which was recommended by the Presentencing Report. It was apparent that my level was set forth due to the court's opinion that I was responsible for all the drugs attributed to my ex-husband.

Ground Two: Ineffective Assistance of Counsel. My due process violation regarding reviewing my PSR and non-evidentiary hearing to determine my role in the offense was not met. I was not afforded the opportunity to review the PSR at least ten days before sentencing.

Ground Three: Post-conviction rehabilitation. I did not want to transition into a halfway house. During my entire time of being incarcerated, I focused on rehabilitating myself to redirect and establish a positive life. I participated in self-help and vocational training programs at Westchester County, and I took a word processing course at FPC, Alderson. I never took typing or word processing in school, not even high school. I read a lot. I must have read over two hundred books. Reading takes your mind out of the place that you are in; you didn't need permission for that. I wrote a letter to my attorney on March 13, 1998, letting him know that I was not satisfied with the reduction and wanted to file a motion to the District Court. Could he please assist? Soon after that, I received a letter dated March 31, 1998, from one of the firm's partners informing me that my attorney was now a Judge of the Superior Court and no longer practiced law. It was suggested that I contact the federal defender's office for assistance.

I filed a motion in March 1999, seeking in pursuant of twenty-eight U.S.C 2255 to vacate, set aside, or correct my sentence. The government asked for an additional sixty days; it was granted. Once the government reviewed my motion, they asked for an additional sixty days. They had not received the transcripts from the Appellant Court; it was July 1999. In October of that same year, I again wrote the court to check my motions' status. It was a stall tactic. If what I was saying was correct in my motions, this was a way to slow the process to keep me in. I ended up doing my seventy-eight months sentence with good time. It came out to sixty-three months, which was five years and three months. In the spring of 2000, I was released to a halfway house in

Hartford, Connecticut. My fight wasn't over; I still had to serve five years of probation. I wrote the judge seeking to terminate my five-year supervised release; I was denied. I served my five years supervised release. I fought to the end.

Chapter 9:

Danbury

Danbury Federal Prison Camp was a much smaller facility. Camp status means the lowest security on the federal level. No cells, and you only had to stand for the count in your room or cubicle. I was always assigned to the top bunk; I didn't want anyone over me. I worked in the kitchen in both facilities. It had its perks, especially if it was something good. Not to mention the hot commodities of access to onions, green peppers, whatever you wanted to add to your fried rice, chilaqueta, and other dishes we could cook in the microwave. Over eighty percent of us were in there for a man. The Black, Latina, and very few Caucasian women were in for drug crimes; most Caucasian women were in there for white-collar crimes such as embezzlement; African women were in there for credit card fraud and checks. The targets were their husbands, boyfriends, brothers, and sons.

Danbury had college courses. You could get a business degree; I had a degree, so I did not qualify. As I watched, talked, and learned about the women around me, so many were uneducated, some had to get a GED in prison, and others had dropped out of high school. Their school was in the streets. Some, like myself, finished but got tangled up in a life that took them off the path. All broken, with low self-esteem, and looking for love in all the wrong places. Some had to make that one run to get money to take care of their children. All and all, they were trying to survive any way they could. I knew, at this point, what I needed to do. I had to get into the schools. Where else was I going to reach a large number of broken girls? I had to give them hope and help build up their self-confidence. I started making plans. I wasn't sure how, but I had to use my life lessons to bless others. Prison was my platform to find my purpose.

Danbury allowed me to see Drew weekly—what a happy-go-lucky, little guy. They traveled, went on a cruise, and had family vacations. If nothing else, he was loved and well rounded. My Mom and Pop kept him busy. Drew and I would do math on the telephone; like me, he liked math. Prison was my time out. I knew he'd understand that concept a lot better than the word prison itself.

On one of his visits to Danbury, he said, "Mommy, what did you do to be in time out? Did you hit somebody?"

I said, "No, I didn't hit anyone."

"Well, did you hurt somebody?"

"No, I didn't hurt anyone."

He's persistent, so he was not going to be satisfied until I eased his conscience. I let him know that he was too young to understand, but I'd tell him once I came home. He said, "I'm old enough to understand." I assured him I'd be home soon, so we'd talk about it then. He was content with my response. I didn't ignore him, and I let him know his question was important to me, and I'd answer when the time was right, but not at that moment.

I started talking about something else to take his mind off my punishment. "When are you coming home? Can I ask the lady over there if you can come home?" he asked as he pointed to the correction officer. So innocent and serious. I had to tell him we'd count on the calendar. He was at the point where you couldn't tell him, he wanted to see for himself. I had less than a year at this point, so each day, he would check the days off his calendar. The closer I got to my release date, we'd count down the days. We were so much alike; at night, instead of watching television, he would draw to wind down. My mother and Pop believed that when you went to your room to go to bed, that's what you did—no television. I was so blessed to have both my mom and Pop—that's what we called my mom's husband. I'm not too fond of the word step-dad or stepfather. Pop was a Christian man; Drew's role model who taught him how to tie a tie. When he died, his whole world crashed.

I went through periods of being in dark spaces and doubts of self-worth in my prison of marriage. Actual prison brought peace and calm to my life. I was able to heal and plan my future. I set goals for myself. My life would finally be mine to direct and control. One evening while in the FPC Danbury, I was awoken by a presence that sat at the foot of my bed. I wasn't startled or scared. It was a sense of love and happiness. I was on the top bunk, and the ladder was up by my waist. I felt a love that only a grandmother could project. She assured me that everything was going to be alright.

"Follow my dreams and don't ever doubt what GOD can do. I am fine and delighted," she told me. "I believe in you, and I am so very proud of you. You are going to do great things, more than you can ever imagine. You will inspire multitudes of people and change the lives of many. I love you. Live in your purpose."

The presence (my maternal grandmother, whom I called Mother) left. I could not fully understand what her presence meant until the next day when my family came to tell me my grandmother, my summer mother, for as long as I could remember, had passed on. My heart was heavy, but I was overwhelmed, knowing that she loved me enough to make her presence known before ascending into heaven. I shed tears and tried to get a pass to attend the funeral, but my request was denied. The feds were not going to spend money and the manpower to take me to North Carolina. I cried, but that was short-lived because I had already had my one last time with her. My memories were more than enough. If I couldn't be there, I'd make my presence known. At that moment, I decided to write a poem that needed to be read at the funeral. A poem that would reflect her role and impact on my life. When the feds said no, I went anyway, not physically, but spiritually, and my presence was felt when my poem was read. No was not an option from my incarceration on.

Chapter 10:

The Transition

When I was released, my plans were set. I was going to move to Maryland in a year. The key to the halfway house was, the sooner you got a job, the sooner you got to go on home confinement.

While at Danbury, the Head Supervisor of the kitchen said, "McCurvin, if we weren't in this situation, me an officer and you an inmate, I'd buy a restaurant and have you run the kitchen. You are so good at holding it down and making my job easier; you take so much pride in what you do."

"I was always taught to be the best at whatever you do." He then went on to tell me about this restaurant, TGI Fridays, that has the best Jack Daniel wings. "Make sure you apply there when you get out."

I applied and was hired the first week I got out. Two weeks later, I was in home confinement. The feds paid for the bed at the halfway house; you too pay a certain percentage of your pay. So the quicker you get out, the quicker they will have room to move someone else into that same spot. Meanwhile, the feds, you, and all that follow you are paying for that bed during your time of home confinement. It could be up to five women paying for the same bed over my four-month time.

I did five years, three months, two days, eight hours, and four minutes inside with no problems. The halfway house staff checked in on me periodically unannounced. One of the stipulations was that you had to have a phone in the room you were staying in; no products could be in your room with alcohol as one of the first three ingredients. I had fingernail polish remover in my bedroom when the staff came by to do a spot check. It had alcohol as one of the first three ingredients; she violated me and took me back to the halfway house. To be this close to full freedom and get violated was more than I was willing to take.

On the way back to the halfway house, she engaged in small talk. I remained silent. By the time we got to Hartford, my mother had called the halfway house supervisor and told her what happened. The resident manager was directed to take me back home. I told the supervisor to call the feds to come to get me. I would rather go back to prison to finish my time. I returned home and was not harassed again.

After completion of the halfway house, I was assigned a federal probation officer. Although the feds do not have probation, I had supervised release and still had to report monthly. I had five years of supervised release. I liked my probation officer; she didn't prejudge me, and she was empathetic when I shared my story. The whole story, because what the papers said did not give a full picture of the truth.

She said, "Antoinette, you got caught up in a bad situation. Now it's time for you to get your life back." The PO asked me to speak to a group of troubled teens. I told her I would love to.

When I met her there, the girls came down all hard, looking at me like I had an extra eye, frowning and making faces. I introduced myself and spoke and began sharing my story. Their whole body language changed; their looks became softer. A few approached me after and hugged me. I let them know that they had their entire lives ahead of them from this day forward, and to make better choices. I then went on to tell them that they would not want to switch places with where I'd been. My PO thanked me. I told her my plan I'd devised in prison to go into the school system. She looked me in my eyes and said, "Antoinette, you will never be able to teach or get a job in the school system." My whole heart dropped; why would GOD put it on my heart if I couldn't do it? One thing I do know is when GOD gives you a dream, it has meaning.

My vision was so clear; I was standing before the multitudes teaching. This dream never ceased; it was continuous. That statement stung for a long time.

It was ten months, and I was ready to leave Connecticut. The house's tension was not good, and I did not want to continue getting into disagreements with my mother, especially in front of Drew. I was thankful for all that she had done for both him and me. But I would not allow her or anyone to yell, curse, or talk down to me ever again. She, of all people, should know how that made one feel. Obviously, she was still angry with me for going to prison and then adding my continuous communication with people I met along the way. I developed bonds with some of these women that I will have for the rest of my life. We all made choices and paid a heavy price; it doesn't define us as bad, it just means we are human.

My mother told me she called the Probation Officer who was over my supervised release, and informed her that I was still communicating with the women I'd met in the halfway house. I spoke to the Probation Officer the next day when I went to check in. She said, "It's human nature that friendships develop. You don't just stop communicating with people; I get it." She then went on to share a story about her best friend. My Probation Officer respected me. She said, "I have supervised many people, and you, by far, are my most straightforward case."

I told her my plans to relocate to Maryland with my line sister, Terri, to get a fresh start. I needed to remove myself from the environment where this all happened. I didn't feel I would get a fair chance if I stayed in the area. I had no idea how this was going to pan out. I knew there had to be a procedure in place, but I was hoping I didn't have to wait five years to move.

She immediately asked, "When do you want to leave?"

In total amazement, I said, "Tomorrow."

Before she could transfer me down to Maryland, I had to secure employment. Meanwhile, I would need to check in with her once a month until I did. I was ecstatic that I could finally go to Maryland. I told my mother and Pop about my conversation with the Probation Officer and that I was leaving. They were okay with it but emphasized that Andrew needed to stay in Connecticut where he was stable until I got my own place. He had his own home here, and to up and disrupt his life was not fair to him. He had been through enough. Moving was a bittersweet moment because I had to leave Drew once again; at least this time, it was to establish a home for us.

Drew and I talked about moving to Maryland before, so it wasn't a surprise when I conversed with him. He agreed to stay in Connecticut as all his friends were there. I promised him that we would talk daily and fly him down during his school breaks. The next day, I packed whatever I had in garbage bags and left for Maryland.

Chapter 11:

Pre-judgement

I transferred my employment with TGI Friday's from Connecticut to Maryland. My managers were sad to see me go but fully understood the need to move on. They called Maryland's TGI Friday's and gave me a verbal recommendation. It was less than a month, and I was then switched over to Maryland for supervision. I was assigned a male PO. He was cocky and judgmental. On his first visit to the house, he asked me if I was a mule because most women were. As he got to know me, he apologized for prejudging me and for making those unprofessional statements. He shared that most of his cases were usually predictable in the same stories, but mine was different.

"You're an educated, articulate woman that got caught up with a drug dealer, so unfortunate in your case." This PO's reaction to me was one that most people have when they hear ex-felon. You are judged without people getting to know the real you.

Chapter 12:

Against All Odds

I went on a field trip to the Board of Education with Terri to drop off paperwork to the certification office. The Board of Education was a busy place that felt like I was in a bus or train station with all the people going back and forth, in and out of offices. As we sat there waiting for her name to be called, a human resources woman stopped and asked if we had our positions for the upcoming school year. Terri said she did and went on to tell her she was here to drop off her coursework she had completed weeks prior. The woman then asked me if I had a job for the fall. I said no. Terri interjected and asked the HR women if an ex-felon could teach. The HR women said yes, as long as the crime was nonviolent and not a crime against a child.

At this point, I wanted to scream. I was on cloud nine. I was told I couldn't, and a hiring agent just confirmed I could. She then said, "Let's go see the head of HR." Once I got into the office, I told him my story. I married a man that sold drugs, and when he went down, he took me down with him. I even explained that if he had plead guilty and not taken it to trial, I wouldn't have done a day.

He said, "Make sure you fill out the application and explain your situation." It was the summer of 2001, less than a year after my release, and I walked into my dream. I secured employment once again, this time with the Board of Education. I had two interviews, one high school and one middle school. I chose the latter of the two. I loved science. How difficult could it be to teach? I learned soon enough that I wasn't teaching science. I was teaching students. I had to get to know them before I could teach the content.

In my first year, I had forty honor students in one class. They were bright and kept me on my toes. One of my girls was pregnant. I went home and cried; a baby was having a baby. I took a nap every day after work, I was so mentally drained. When you give so much of yourself, your energy becomes depleted. None of that mattered, though, because I was walking in my purpose. The purpose that people said I could never do. I knew that day, and every day after that, what's for me was for me.

I became a professional over the years. I knew that to perfect my craft, I needed to participate in professional development to build my capacity. I finished my educational requirement within the allotted time, but the Praxis was my kryptonite. Test anxiety, phobia, I panicked with test-taking. I took and passed Pedagogy on my first go-round with flying colors. I had to write a biology lesson if I remember correctly; it was a piece of cake. Praxis II took a couple of times; I passed math next to science, that was my favorite subject.

On the other hand, I failed Praxis II, my content, nine times. Can you imagine failing the content your degree is in, not once or twice, but nine times? I took all my assessments at an HBCU. On my tenth time, I decided to change venues and changed my ethnicity from African American to Other; I passed.

I was overjoyed—not sure if I jumped up and down or if I did a cartwheel. I had spent the past school year as a per diem teacher due to my certification deadline not being met. It was a rough year having to pay for my own health insurance through Cobra; I had to pass, there was no other option. My certification was my one roadblock stopping me from buying a home for both Drew and me. Once I received my scores, I took all my paperwork to the Board of Education. When my certification came in, I was official. I not only secured employment with the district, but I was also a certified teacher.

Chapter 13:

The Earthquake

The Probation Officer had become a regular at my house. He was no longer just supervising my release; he became an associate. His visit this day was one that I will never forget. He told Terri and I that he was bragging to his colleagues about me and how I was his most manageable caseload; I was a teacher doing well. He then found himself defending me to them. His supervisor wanted to know how an ex-felon could be a teacher. My PO was then instructed to call the Board of Education to make sure they knew. He then told me he had to call, and he apologized a million times.

I was hurt. Here I was getting my life back in order, and the feds wanted to stop my progress. I immediately called my hiring agent at the Board of Education and shared what the PO had mentioned. He told me to resign quietly before a big blow-up occurred. I told the hiring agent that I would not resign. I never lied on my application, and he hired me.

I was scared at this point, not sure what was going to happen. All I knew was I was honest. I contacted my mentor, Assistant Principal C.

He was calm as always, and he looked me in my eyes and said, "Mack." That's what he always called me; short for McCurvin. "It's not about prison, the FEDS, or the Board of Education; it's about you. How are you going to handle this situation? You were honest and hired. To ease your conscience, I'm going to give you my attorney's number; call and make an appointment to see him. My attorney will tell you what you need to do."

I went to see the attorney. I explained my truth. He asked, "Did you answer yes on your application?"

I said, "Yes."

"And they still hired you?"

"Yes."

After that, his exact words were, "If they fire you, you have a case. Do not resign, or if it blows up, let it, but they can say whatever they want. If they fire you, we're going to be rich." I smiled and then laughed. He made my day.

I was contacted by the Board of Education to come in and do fingerprints again. I don't know what they thought would change from the first time I did them until now, but I went. My prints were sent out. They again came back with no findings for the forty plus charges listed.

I gave my PO a copy of the results. He then apologized again and said I would never be bothered about this matter again. All that played over in my head since my hiring date, and I knew that it was God. I wish I could say that this was the end of my woes down at the Board of Education.

I was a master teacher for the state of Maryland. The state had adopted the Common Core State Standards and the Next Generation Science Standards, so each district would recommend their elite teachers to travel to the different districts to facilitate professional development for these new standards. I was away at one of the conferences when I received a phone call from my principal. He asked why I hadn't told him I was leaving. I was puzzled.

"What do you mean? I'm not leaving."

My principal then went on to say technology had contacted him and told him to make sure I turned in my laptop. I had no idea what was going on. The first thing that came to mind was, *Is this a tactic to get me out?* Did I get fired and not know about it? I immediately called my mentor Assistant Principal, panicking because I was fired somehow and was not informed.

He told me to calm down, call the attorney when I got back in town, and he'd take it from there. The next day when I got back, I went straight to the Board of Education demanding answers. The HR representative over my school looked at the computer, left her office, went over to a colleague's computer in the main office, and said something that I couldn't hear. They both looked at the computer, then back at me. Someone had put down that I was leaving the county and going to another district as the reason for me leaving. I had no clue what they were talking about. I wasn't leaving, nor was I going to another district. I needed to know how this could happen. The individual would have to have had access to my private information. How could this be? The HR representative then said she must have done it, transposed some number, and put me in instead of another employee. I didn't buy it. I called security services and explained to them what happened. I needed them to investigate and find out what computer this transaction took place on.

The investigator promised me that he would look into it and get back to me. After the investigation, it was found that the transaction took place in human resources. The human resources representative was telling the truth, after all. Nonetheless, how negligent can one be to create such chaos? I later found out that everyone in the human resources office had to reapply for their jobs. My human resources representative was one of the ones that was dismissed. The day I came in was her last day. I often wonder if it was deliberate since she was on her way out. That incident had me on pins and needles.

As the science department chairperson over the years, my ultimate goal was to bring science to life in the classrooms. Our biggest hurdle as a district was getting the students up to par with the Maryland State Assessment in Science. It was three years of science on one test. We had no idea what we were in for, and the scores told the story. I knew there had to be a way to master these standards and maintain the knowledge over the three years. I would go online and pull the practice tests and make transparencies for the teachers to use as warm-ups. Using the transparencies became a yearly procedure. Each teacher had a binder full of transparencies that they used to review prior years' standards during the warm up time. It took four years before we became proficient. Keep in mind those students had to test in fifth grade, so they were familiar with the test coming into middle school.

The task was met now. My goal was for my school to score higher than the district overall. We reviewed the standards and maintained the same system put into place. Not only did we achieve proficiency, but we also kept a higher score than the district. The state later adopted the Next Generation Science Standards, which were geared toward the twenty-first century focus to include engineering. Little did I know that years later, this would be my dissertation focus.

As my out of the classroom roles were becoming more administrative and supervisory, I decided to pursue my Master's degree. The district had partnerships with neighboring colleges and universities. The flexibility and convenience were perfect for a working mother.

It took me two years from start to finish to complete my Master's at Coppin State University. Seeking a degree as a working mother was much more meaningful than when I was a young adult. The degree was a status change in addition to a pay increase. With a Master's degree, I was eligible for other positions. I graduated from Coppin in 2009.

After my move to Maryland in February 2001, I bought a car and house within the same year. It was time for Drew to come to Maryland. Pop passed away the same year Drew was supposed to move to Maryland. I had to make another tough decision. My mom had lost Pop; what was going to happen when I took Drew? He kept her busy. I left him there another year. It was his worst school year ever. When I would visit the school on my breaks, the teacher would ask if he could come with me because that's all he talked about. I assured her that he would be coming with me after this school year.

The summer leading into his eighth-grade school year, Drew moved to Maryland. We were finally together again, and this time for good. Drew was diagnosed with juvenile diabetes when he was six. I needed him to be with me, not at the neighborhood school. I received special permission for him to come to my school. When Drew graduated from Riverdale Baptist, he asked if he could go to a prep school before college. He was a young senior as he'd entered school at the age of four. Both he and I agreed that an extra year to mature would do him well. We visited several prep schools. Valley Forge Military Academy offered us a scholarship, and we took it. It was forty-plus thousand a year. Although the mountains scared me, I was at every football game, whether home or away.

Chapter 14:

Ongoing Challenges

Once I got out, proving myself was a constant factor. The title ex-felon holds a stigma. People judge you without even knowing the whole truth. The newspapers and Google display a one-sided perspective of the government's side. It doesn't tell you about the abuse and all the other factors that contributed to my involvement.

I sought and received a real estate license when I got to Maryland. I had already started the process in Connecticut, but different states required a different number of hours. I lived in Silver Spring, and there was a well-known agency right on Route 29. I went to that agency, and the office manager told me I could take the courses there free since I had already done most of them in Connecticut; I would need to sit for all of Maryland's requirements.

When I went to take my real estate exam, I failed one of the parts (there I go again with the test-taking). Once I retook the test, I passed. To get my license, I had to answer that dreaded question. Have you ever been convicted? I replied, yes. Instead of receiving my real estate license in the mail, I was asked to come to the Baltimore, Maryland, real estate commissioner office. *Oh Lordy, I am going on trial again*, is what I kept thinking. When I arrived, I was led to a big conference room with real estate board members and the commissioner sitting facing me and a stenographer—talk about Deja Vu. I sat and faced the group. I thought about Tupac's "All Eyes on Me" song sitting there.

"We noticed you answered yes to being convicted. Would you elaborate?" they asked. I shared that I was married to a man who sold drugs, and when he went down, I went down.

One of the members asked, "Why didn't you leave?"

I replied, "I was young, naïve, and in love."

Another member asked, "Do you have children?"

My reply was, "Yes, we have a son together."

My emotions came to the surface. All that I had been through in my marriage, being incarcerated away from my son, and now here I was fighting to get my life back. I stood up and said, "I stand convicted of the crime charged. I was incarcerated in federal prison, the price society demanded. I did my time—all of it. I just want to get on with my life. I do not want this to be held over my head for the rest of my life."

I left, not knowing where I stood, but I had spoken my truth. I let them know that I did not want to keep paying for a crime I had already paid the ultimate price for. By Friday of that same week, my real estate license was in the mail.

Chapter 15:

Being a Parent

As a parent, we aren't given a book of steps to take or the best way to raise your child. We are all amateurs and do the best that we know how to do. The child is a reflection of his or her parents. Children do what they see because it's all they know. As an educator, I see so many angry children. My first thought is, *Why?* Or do I know why? Is there abuse in the home, yelling, cursing, and belittling? All of this negative interaction destroys a child's self-esteem at such a young age. The comment that always seems to get under my skin is when a mother says "You are just like your father." I never understood what that meant. DNA doesn't lie. But if you are saying it as a negative gesture, the child didn't choose his father—you did. I married my father. I married an abusive man, a womanizer, and a drug dealer. The difference between my dad and my ex-husband was that my dad loved me beyond what words could say. He didn't bring his street life home, nor did it affect anyone but him.

To my ex-husband, I was a trophy for display. His love for me became control and obsession, ending with his determination for me to be confined while he was incarcerated. He'd rather I be in prison than on the street with another man; at that point, he'd lose control.

I missed Drew's first day of school, all the monumental events in his life that I would only get to experience in a picture. This drug world wasn't fair, not even to the children that became collateral damage. I was blessed to have my mother and Pop. I was at peace knowing that he was being raised by the woman that gave me life. We didn't always get along, but she loved me at the end of the day and never gave up on me. My guilt was undeniably overwhelming after all that I put my family through. I'd lay in my bunk at night crying and thinking about Drew; he didn't deserve to be without his mommy. A flood of emotions consumed me in my early days, but I knew if I wanted to be a better mother and woman when I walked out of prison, I had to start focusing on finding myself again.

Chapter 16:

Writing Retreat

It was 2020 and I was still struggling to write this book. Every time I sit down and write, my mind and emotions go back to that time, and the tears flow uncontrollably, so I stop. People say it helps with the healing process, and knowing that my journey may be the inspiration others need to push through is my motivation to finish.

To get over, I had to go through every pain and emotion. *Lord, please help me to stay on task.* I came to North Virginia Beach away from the boardwalk that I once hung out at during Labor Day weekend during my college days. This was, as I called it, a dig deeper solo writing retreat. I have this book in me that has to get out. Too many sad days. It's like a pungent smell that won't go away. Have you ever cried so hard that the muscles in your stomach ache? That's the cry I've had since last week. The cry that says, *please release this pain.*

This morning as I watched the sunrise; some of the pain was let go. Damn, that's deep, and just like that, the ocean came up toward me and retracted back in the opposite direction. A little weight was lifted.

Wow, this feels good. Can't wait to come back out in the morning to release more. Our body is composed of sixty percent water; water is calming but can also be fierce, especially a tsunami—an underwater earthquake or volcanic eruption that causes humongous waves that can wipe out a whole island. Amazing, right? The very thing that we need to survive in its natural state can kill us once displaced. Powerful beyond measure!

The ocean and the sound of the waves are so serene. It helps me open and release. Every morning I would go out about 5:30 a.m., waiting for the sun to rise. The moment a dense red behind the clouds would appear, I jumped up like a child excited about going to the amusement park. I got dressed and hurried downstairs, not wanting to miss the sunrise. The hallway was quiet. The building was quiet. It was as if I was the only person stirring. Thank God I brought my mini-sized flashlight as the beach was still dark. I didn't want to step on anything. I decided to walk straight ahead and not stray too far; after all, it was dark and I had to stay safe. Thirty minutes had passed before people began coming out, so I felt more comfortable walking down the beach; social distancing was not an issue here. On my first night, I ate dinner outside on the patio of the restaurant. Lovely set up, all tables were six feet apart, if not more. The view of the ocean right there. I was at my happy place after the completion of this book. I want my mind to stay right in this moment.

My prison experience made me realize that there is good in everything.

No matter the situation, there is a positive outcome within our reach. The most important factor is learning from our trials and tribulations and realizing that they are essential to our growth. "Still I Rise" by Maya Angelou is a powerful poem; I find so much connection to it.

Prison was not only my way out; it forced me to dig deep within. It was an opportunity to heal. There was no more being disconnected from my soul. The Coronavirus lockdown pandemic forced us to face ourselves. It was like the universe gave us permission and time to regroup, refocus on things in our lives we needed to change. The perfect opportunity for us to use our time wisely and finally develop a plan on how we would move forward with our goals; goals we could not seem to find the time to pursue. At this time, it didn't matter how much money you had—billion-dollar status or homeless. We were all in the same boat. Humanity at its best as we all united to do our part to stop the spread.

I had applied to become an assistant principal many times in the past, but to no avail. One thing I've learned is you don't move to the next level until you are ready. As I look back on my first attempts, I hadn't experienced enough to prepare me for the task of being an assistant principal. There was still so much I didn't know about the role. Classroom management was one thing, but dealing with all that comes with the position was another. While dealing with the public—good, bad, or indifferent—you have to know what to say and how to say it. This is one profession that if your heart isn't in it, you definitely couldn't do it with fidelity.

Years ago, when I first pursued an assistant principal position, I was qualified on paper but didn't have enough experience. There are different levels and steps I would need to experience to understand the role entirely. Once I became an assistant principal, I was ready. A new wave of energy entered my life, and changes began to happen; things started to align with my dream. After all, to become the CEO of my STEM Magnet Academy, I needed to be in an administrative position.

My passion for science has always been my driving force in education. Throughout my twenty-year tenure in the school system, I have exposed my students to endless science opportunities. My goal was always to promote STEM and get as many students as possible interested in STEM careers. Some events that we participated in were The Black Engineering of the Year Awards (BEYA) Conference in Washington, D.C.; Certified X-STEM School part of the U.S. Science and Engineering Festival hosting scientists that looks like them, which was to inspire students to pursue careers in STEM; Partnerships with NASA; Partnership with Patriots which is a non-for-profit STEM organization; Cybersecurity Completion; Environmental Justice Competition Field trips to the Patent and Trade Office Museum; and I also took twenty-three students to the Women and Minorities STEM Conference on Capitol Hill, Washington, D.C.

In education, I see so many angry children, girls with low self-esteem, and boys who are always on the defense. Is there abuse in their homes? If parents only knew the long-term effects their actions have on their children, I wonder if they would change. Generational curses are real.

That child who comes to school cursing, yelling, and hitting others is only mimicking what they see. Is punishment the answer, or do we need to get to the root of the problem to find the best solution? My heart goes out to the broken children. I was one.

In 2 Corinthians 1 3-5, the apostle Paul was a great encourager who said that we can reach out to others with the comfort that we are comforted by God. In order to experience comfort and have it flow through us, we must first suffer some heartache. There is power in the touch of a person who has been in the valley. A person who experiences pain does not offer empty words, but hope. The most effective encouragers are those who have suffered much. There are only certain principles that can be learned through suffering. At that point, we will be useful to others. God builds encouragers from those who were once broken.

Chapter 17:

Not Every Caterpillar Turns

Into a Butterfly

As I reflect on my past, it was excruciating for me because I had to go back to a place of darkness and fear. I was a broken girl who became a broken and abused woman. Although I wore a smile, I felt empty and unhappy. The physical scars sometimes go away, but hurtful words, especially the demeaning ones, stay with you and become your belief. I was a woman who appeared to be one hundred percent together. A woman who never loved herself more than she showered love onto others. A woman that didn't think she deserved more than she allowed herself to receive. A woman who endured more than the average person could ever bear. Yet I fought my way out of the generational curse I was born into. You see, I've made many bad decisions in my life, but one decision I made was not to stay in bondage.

Transforming into the person you are becoming is a process. The power in the transition is in the dark space. When you have hit rock bottom, there is a drive within to move from that position. You decide what direction you will go. To deal with my bondage, I had to identify its origin. I had to dig deep within to find the source of my pain. In doing so, I had to take ownership of my actions, and it was at that moment that I became free. Imagine being bound your entire life and not realizing you transitioned from one form of bondage to another. I have my life back, a life that I am the CEO of—no one else. Life has been full of challenges, but the struggle is only a struggle if you give up.

My life journey has proven that giving up is not an option. The essence of time well spent helped me experience peace and pushed me to my positive potential. By spending my time wisely, I was able to break out of my inner prison. Rock bottom for me wasn't prison; it was my marriage. Even when I lost, I've always won. Prison not only saved my life, but it was also my bridge to freedom. Everyone has a superpower, and mine is called perseverance. What is yours?

"Every Caterpillar doesn't change into a butterfly..."

Dr. Antoinette M. Glenn

About the Author

Education Consultant, Author, Speaker

Dr. Antoinette Glenn, is the CEO of Impactful Educational Consulting LLC. She is a published author and speaker. Dr. Glenn has a signature program entitled Empowerment Principles that Transforms Professionals. Her speaking topics are Obstacle based empowerment, Expectation based empowerment, Blueprint based empowerment and Belief based empowerment

Dr. Glenn has been in education for over 19 years. Serving in roles as a science educator, Science Department Chairperson, STEM Coordinator, STEM Instructional Lead Teacher, Master Teacher for the state of Maryland, curriculum writer, and currently an Assistant Principal. Dr. Glenn has presented at district, state and national science conferences. She has a published article entitled "The Impact of the Middle School Transition on the Science Achievement Gap." Dr. Glenn has presented at her Alma mater Virginia State University the topic was STEM is more valuable than salt. She has also served as a panelist for Black Women and STEM at Virginia Commonwealth University (VCU).

She earned a Bachelor of Science (B.S.) in Pre-Medical Biology at Virginia State University, a Master of Science (M.S.) in Adult and General Education with a specialty in Administration and Supervision at Coppin State University and a Doctorate of Education degree in Educational Policy, Planning and Leadership with a focus in Executive K-12 Administration from the College of William and Mary. Dr. Glenn is driven by the desire to inspire, motivate, and develop others. She is the proud member of Delta Sigma Theta Sorority, Incorporated, and the National Council of Negro Women, Inc.

Made in the USA
Middletown, DE
16 November 2021